The Awakening and the Calling of the Holy Spirit

Darla Colombo

The Awakening and the Calling of the Holy Spirit

By Darla Colombo
Illustrations By Dorothy Swick

XULON PRESS

Xulon Press
2301 Lucien Way #415
Maitland, FL 32751
407.339.4217
www.xulonpress.com

© 2023 by Darla Colombo

Illustrated by: Dorothy Swick
Contribution by: Pastor Sheldon Nickerson

All rights reserved solely by the author. The author guarantees all contents are original and do not infringe upon the legal rights of any other person or work. No part of this book may be reproduced in any form without the permission of the author.

Due to the changing nature of the Internet, if there are any web addresses, links, or URLs included in this manuscript, these may have been altered and may no longer be accessible. The views and opinions shared in this book belong solely to the author and do not necessarily reflect those of the publisher. The publisher therefore disclaims responsibility for the views or opinions expressed within the work.

Unless otherwise indicated, Scripture quotations taken from the King James Version (KJV) – *public domain*.

Scripture quotations taken from the Holy Bible, New Living Translation (NLT). Copyright ©1996, 2004, 2007 by Tyndale House Foundation. Used by permission of Tyndale House Publishers, Inc.

Scripture quotations taken from the Amplified Bible Classic Addition (AMPC). Copyright © 1987 by The Lockman Foundation. Used by permission. All rights reserved

Scripture quotations taken from the New King James Version (NKJV). Copyright © 1982 by Thomas Nelson, Inc. Used by permission. All rights reserved.

Scripture taken from The Passion Translation (TPT). Copyright © 2017 by Passion & Fire Ministries, Inc. Used by permission. All rights reserved. thePassionTranslation.com

Paperback ISBN-13: 978-1-66286-446-9
Ebook ISBN-13: 978-1-66286-447-6

A special thank you to Pastor Sheldon Nickerson of Covenant Church, Fairmont, WV, for his time and technical support. Your skills and wisdom were crucial for the completion of this book.

Table of Contents

Introduction ix

Part 1 Praise / Thanksgiving 1

Part 2 Spirit to the Body 17

Part 3 Warnings 57

Part 4 Holy Spirit's Lessons / Words 95

Prayer 109

Biography of Illustrator, Dorothy Swick 117

INTRODUCTION

The calling of the Holy Spirit is unique and different for each child of the King. As we grow and mature, that calling will change. The key to knowing and understanding your talents is LISTENING to the voice of the Spirit - the greater your faith ... the greater your ministry! Just as God's creativity is beyond our comprehension, so are the gifts that lie just below the surface. As we pray, wait, and obey, the Holy Spirit designs each son and daughter's unique path into the next level of growth. Stepping into that new door, we mature and become more Christ-like in all areas.

In my first book, <u>My Journey with the Lord</u>, I talked about Ephesians 2:10. "For we are His workmanship, created in Christ Jesus for good works, which God prepares beforehand that we should walk in them." NKJV In this verse the word, workmanship, is the Greek word, 'poiema', where we get the English word, poem or poetry. In the Greek language poiema means 'something made'. Just as a poem is an expression of man's creativity, so is mankind a creation made by God Himself. We were designed by a loving Father to be a living light, a living testimony of YAHWEH. We, you and I, are a poem created by the Master. Encased in that creation are gifts, talents, and skills that become a work of art in our Lord's hands.

Exciting and sometimes overwhelming, each day in the Lord is new. Why you may ask? It is to help us become totally dependent on the One who has called each of us to come up higher. In Him we become and be. In Him we can do great exploits that bring Yahweh honor and glory. In Him we can accomplish anything that in the natural seems impossible. Never fear, never doubt, but just know that when He asks you to do something beyond your natural talents, He will give you the grace to succeed and to be successful. Just look up and see the face of your Father. His love will equip you for this new level of glory.

This is a lesson that I have had to learn and relearn. Trusting is difficult when you see in the physical realm obstacles that must be overcome. However, I have finally realized that with my God nothing, absolutely nothing, is impossible! In the natural I have entirely no talent for writing poetry, but the Spirit does. He has a voice for the world today; and if you listen to that still small voice, you will hear Him speaking. Some of these poems have come quickly, and others have taken more time and discernment. Waiting is not always easy but with waiting comes great rewards. Listening, obeying, and believing are the three key commandments given to the body today. Choose to BELIEVE!

PURPLE ~ Royalty, Priesthood, Noble One

PART ONE

Praise and Thanksgiving

"Give thanks to the Lord and proclaim His greatness. Let the whole world know what He has done. Sing to Him; yes, sing His praises. Tell everyone about His wonderful deeds."

1 Chronicles 16:8-10 NLT

Indeed it came to pass, when the trumpeters and singers were as one, to make one sound to be heard in praising and thanking the Lord, and when they lifted up their voice with the trumpets and cymbals and instruments of music, and praised the Lord, saying:

> "For He is good, For His mercy endures forever," that the house, the house of the Lord, was filled with a cloud, 14so that the priests could not continue ministering because of the cloud; for the glory of the Lord filled the house of God.

2 Chron. 5:13-14 AMPC

YAHWEH

Yahweh, You are All-Knowing, All-Powerful, All-Consuming
You look upon Your creation with great love and kindness
You are the only living being Who always was and always will be.

You are true purity – the purest of love
Your holiness encompasses every created being
No one can fathom Your intelligence, Your wisdom, Your imagination

You, Yahweh, are liquid Light that moves in and through every dark region of the universe
Your dunamis power and authority are incomprehensible and cannot be contained
One thought, one word and the universe is forever changed and transformed

Your goodness knows no bounds
You rule with righteous judgements that none can deny
You lift up and bring low
You bless and make new

As this new era dawns
Your chosen ones enter into the fullness of Your plan
Mounting up, they become saturated with wisdom and power
Walking in the authority of the Most High God,
Yahweh

Blossoming

Just as the land of Israel is blossoming again,
So will My Church rise on the foundation that I have planted
New growth, new holiness, new power
If I said it, will I not accomplish it?

Seeds that once lay dormant will now ascend out of the ashes
Justice and righteousness will be established
Come see the fulfillment of the promise
For as of days of old, My Hand is upon this earth
Planting, plucking, pruning until … all that is left is pure LIGHT.

Water coming down from the Heavenly Throne Room
Will bring healing and restoration to all who call upon My Name
Watch and see the Power and the Glory of My Presence
Sweep away all doubt and all unbelief
For the Great I AM is still on the throne
Yesterday, today, and forever My Word shall stand
Nothing, absolutely nothing, can separate Me from My sons and daughters.

The end time church has begun
Just as in the days of Pentecost while My disciples waited and prayed
So shall My new outpouring saturate all who are ready
Filled with Spirit-led anointing, they shall smash the very gates of Hell
Establishing My Kingdom for the soon returning King of Kings and
Lord of Lords
YESHUA!

Oh, Righteous One

The righteous will stand and mount up
They will be lifted above the storms
As they ascend to My Holy Mountain.
With eagles' wings they shall soar
Plucking the lost from the jaws of death
Seeing eyes reveal what the enemy has hidden
All is exposed before My Mighty Sons and Daughters.
ELOHIM's Warriors stand side by side with the Angelic Host
The shofar has sounded …
Announcing the dawn of the righteousness of God being restored.

Tremble, shake, you demonic spirits
Look up … see the Lion of the tribe of Judah roar
Fall on your face and bow down, for no evil can stand before the Great I AM!
The battle will be won by the weapons of Light
Anointed, spirit-filled believers will never tire
They stand with the Sword of the Spirit, wreaking havoc on the plans of the enemy.

So Arise you Mighty Warriors, equipped with the Armor of God
Come forth … the Lord of Heavens' Army awaits.
Take your position and move out
Hear the trembling sound of the demons, for they know the battle has already been won
How? By the Blood of the Lord, Yeshua, the Messiah!

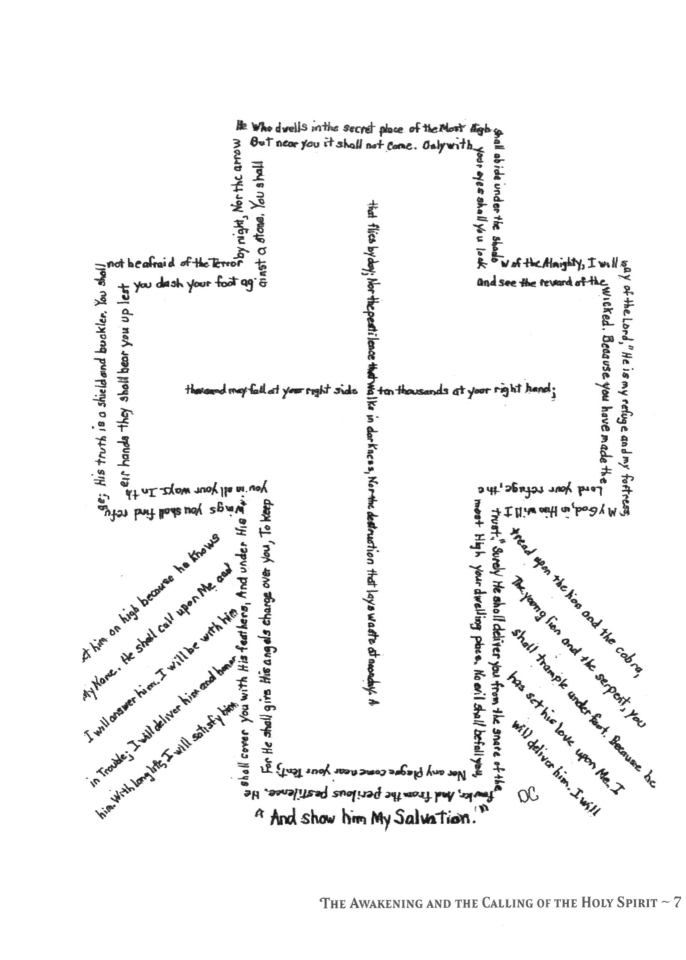

The Awakening and the Calling of the Holy Spirit ~ 7

Thanksgiving

My heart swells in gratitude to You, Lord
Just a touch from You restores my soul
Filling me with overwhelming pure love
Soaking into my inner man
Bringing peace, joy, happiness, rest

Father how can I ever thank You for this great love?
Freely You came, and freely You give
Never looking back but only forward
Laying aside Your Kingship to be a servant
Pouring out everything so I could be free.
Free to enter into Your throne room
Free to enter Your Presence
Free to be changed and given new birth
Free to be a son or daughter of the Most High

Thank You, oh Holy One
Let Your love encompass me
So that I can love others unconditionally
So that I can draw water from the well
Living water that heals, restores, and saves.
Holy and Righteous are You Lord
Worthy of all praise and adoration … worthy, worthy, worthy
Is my Savior, my Friend, my Anchor … JEHOVAH!

PURE

Without spot or wrinkle
Without sin
Without hatred
Without falsehood
Without deception
Without greed
Without deceit
Without darkness
Without lack
Without bitterness
Without turning
Without unforgiveness
Without pride
Without arrogance
Without limit
Without corruption
Without defilement
Without flaws
Without EVIL
Adonai Elohim

MAJESTY

How majestic are Your ways Lord
How holy are Your truths
As the waters beckon to Your call
So does each child hearken to Your voice.

Stir the fire, Lord
Cleanse and purify until breakthrough comes
As the potter fashions clay into a work of art,
So are Your sons and daughters molded into useful vessels.
As the wheel spins, glimpses of transformed lives appear
Extreme heat burns up all impurities
Leaving the purest holiness that radiates LOVE.

Now Your chosen ones are ready
Now the enemy has no foothold
A shofar sounds and a cry is heard, "Come forth!"
Standing at attention, the soldiers are given their mission by their
Commander-in-Chief
Fully equipped, God's Army moves into position
As the shaking begins, the Mighty Warriors break strongholds
Releasing those held bound
Declaring the Majesty and Power of their God!

The Brightness of God's Glory

No sickness, no pain, no fear, no lack
When God's Glory rest upon His children
Eye has not seen nor has ear heard the wonders the Almighty has for each one.

God's Glory brings refreshment and joy; rest for weary bodies; healing for broken spirits
A Light so radiant that it pierces the very heart of mankind
Shedding lies and deceptions planted by the enemy.

As new sprouts emerge out of winter's lifeless ground
So does man come alive as God's Glory pierces his soul.
What once seemed dead begins to quicken life
Tiny seedlings of the Word dig deep into the fallow soil of the heart
Suddenly, a new awakening and new growth pierce the very core of mankind
Filling this new life with the Glory of the Father.

Dry, dead bones come together as the Spirit hovers
A fresh wind of the Father breathes on each dry bone
Saturating and sealing this new generation of believers.
A Mighty Army of Saints stands at attention!

The Lord speaks from His Heavenly Throne, "Come! Take your position and go forth.
Destroy the enemy's plan and release the captives!
My Glory is your Way Maker and Strong Tower.
My Light illuminates the darkest regions of Sheol and exposes the tactics of the evil one.
Go Forth Mighty Ones!
I AM has spoken and I AM will perform My WORD!"

Hallelujah, Hallelujah, Hallelujah

Hallelujah, Yeshua is Spirit and Truth
Those who worship the Lord must worship Him
In His Spirit and in His truth
Blinded eyes are opened when the Holy One's Truth floods each heart.

There are two doors from which to enter
Chose the One that leads to Life
As you step inside, God's Glory will appear
Draw close to that Light, and all darkness will flee!

Rest in His Presence as peace permeates your soul
His truth will saturate your entire being
Allow your Daddy to mold you and restore you
Become that child the Creator destined you to be.

Then you will walk in divine knowledge
Then discernment will settle and remain upon you
Then your light will radiate and shine on all who come in your presence
Then God's glory will cover you!

God's Glory

Mighty Glory

Lasting Glory

Righteous Glory

Resurfacing Glory

Insurmountable Glory

Resting Glory

Beautiful Glory

Creation's Glory

Birthing Glory

Holy Glory

Saturating Glory

Commanding Glory

Healing Glory

Saving Glory

Unspeakable Glory

Merciful Glory

Comforting Glory

Perfect Glory

God IS Glory

Blessings and Honor

Blessings and Honor are always Yours, Lord
For You alone are the Most Holy and deserve all of our praise
We thank You for being ADONAI, the Lord our God
For being our Father and our Savior
Your Word is established in the heavens
And is settled in the earth
As the lightning flashes across the sky, so is Your Word
It is a lamp unto our feet and wisdom to our souls
It is the foundation of all that is holy
It is unmovable and sealed by the blood
Your Shekinah rests upon Your Word, declaring Your Truth.

May Your Name be honored and elevated
Holy, Holy, Holy is the Name that is above all names
At Your Name, Yeshua, everything that can be named must bow
For Your Name is Purity and Holiness
It floods the deep recesses of our souls
Transforming each child into a Warrior
Let Your Spirit draw us and fill us
Saturate Your children with the oil that flows from Your Heavenly Throne
Moving in and through us, establishing I AM's will for our lives
Hallelujah, Hallelujah to our King
The robe of Your Majesty fills the temple, declaring the greatness of
Your Glory!

JEHOVAH SHALOM

Joyful
Wonderful
Restful
Healing
PEACE
Poured out on all who will receive.
Flowing from the Throne Room of God
This glorious PEACE saturates each child.
As it flows from the Presence of a loving Father
Moving in, throughout, and around
This PEACE knows no bounds.
Its oil never stops, never lacks
But wraps each son and daughter in a cocoon of love
Where no evil can abide.
Only the pure love of Jehovah
Gives rest
Gives life
Gives hope
Jehovah Shalom
The Lord of PEACE!

GREEN ~ Life, Restoration, Growth

PART TWO

Spirit to the Body

"Wisdom is a gift from God, and every word He speaks is full of revelation and becomes a fountain of understanding within you."

Proverbs 2:6 TPT

Let me emphasize this: As you yield to the dynamic life and power of the Holy Spirit, you will abandon the cravings of your self-life. 17When your self-life craves the things that offend the Holy Spirit you hinder him from living free within you! And the Holy Spirit's intense cravings hinder your self-life from dominating you! So then, the two incompatible and conflicting forces within you are your self-life of the flesh and the new creation life of the Spirit.

18But when you yield to the life of the Spirit, you will no longer be living under the law, but soaring above it!

Gal. 5:16-18 TPT

MY LITTLE ONES

Awake My little ones
Look around … see into the spiritual realm
There's a tearing and a pulling down
A separating … the old gives way to the new

Light breaks forth through the darkness, radiating across the earth
Purity, holiness, righteousness begin to grow
As seeds of the Word are planted in the soil of man's heart

Men and women emerge out of confusion
With a fresh anointing of TRUTH
Scales of blindness start to dissolve
As the oil of the Spirit flows

A suddenly takes root,
As the breath of the Spirit blows across the
dormant field of souls
Bringing life and resurrection to each son and daughter

Now you are ready
Step into My Presence and look down from My position
Then you can see clearly
I've given you the authority to break and to restore
GO forth now and bring My Will into existence!

The Sound Intensifies

A sound is heard
Calling sons and daughters back
To the feet of their Savior, Jesus.

A new season demands new oil
The oil from yesterday has lost its flavor.
Pure oil is only found in His Presence
Where peace, joy, happiness, and rest
Are infused into each child of the King.

This sound intensifies deep inside mankind's spirit
Drawing and leading the Lord's chosen ones
Back to the foot of the cross
Where a spirit of humility and obedience is formed.

This new oil is only found resting in Yahweh's arms
He is calling His children back to a place of intimacy
Won't you come home?
Your Lord, your Savior, your Friend
Awaits!

Come See

God's Mighty Army
Shifting into position
Releasing the POWER

Transformation, Wholeness
Spirit, Soul, Body
Harken to His Voice
God is not late; God is not slack

Every WORD written by the Spirit
WILL come to pass
Heed the warning
DON'T BACK DOWN

Stand, Speak, Declare
His uncompromising Truth
Decree God's perfect Will
Over each situation, each soul
DON'T BACK DOWN

Know the Lord listens
His angelic warriors heed His Voice
DON'T BACK DOWN, DON'T BACK DOWN
VICTORY has already been WON!

MIGHTY WARRIOR

Rise up, oh mighty warrior
You are fully equipped for battle.
I have prepared the way for your victory
March into the enemy's territory and take back all that was stolen.
Set the captives FREE!

Open prison doors in the deepest region of Hell
Use the Sword of My Spirit, the Word of God
Break every chain that has ensnared My sons and daughters.

Look up … do you not see My Angelic Army that fights with you?
Nothing, absolutely nothing, can harm you
Why … because the Lord God lives inside you.
When you speak My Word, I AM speaks!
When you battle, I AM battles!

Spirit come … fill My warriors with fire and oil
Burn and consume until nothing is left but Me!
Watch now as My army moves into position
Only the Word is needed
The captives are released as the Lion of the tribe of Judah ROARS!

TURNING

Turning … turning
My Hand is changing the atmosphere
Can you feel it?
Can you see it?

BLOW wind … let My Spirit sweep away
All that is not rooted in Me
All that the enemy has planted

Righteousness arise!
Justus be established!
For My Word shall STAND

Darkness must flee
Deception must bow down
Every demonic plan shall be exposed
As the breath of My Spirit
Whirls, lifts, and uncovers
All lies, all strongholds

WATCH … see them crash
Broken into pieces that cannot be rebuilt
Only that which is birth in Me
Shall be left STANDING!

LISTEN TO THE VOICE

Listen to the voice of the Holy Spirit
Stand in the gap and watch
Declare and decree God's Word, and it shall be confirmed
Those who are prepared and ready
Will move out in the Lord's Anointing
Shaking the very gates of Hell

Listen, can you hear it?
A mighty rushing wind, sweeping away all that entangles
All that deceives
All that usurps the will of Adonai

As the Church takes her place,
Restoration continues
A spirit of unity envelops the Bride of Christ

Moving into the highways and by-ways
The Bride in union with the Lord
Heals the sick, raises the dead, casts out the demonic
Righteousness is restored
Justice is established
Holiness is reclaimed!

CALLED

Today I have called you
I have sealed you with My Spirit
As the sun rises in the east
And sets in the west
So is the foundation on which
You have been planted.

As the Spirit leads, you must follow
As the Spirit speaks, you must speak.
I have given you a voice
To proclaim My Word in this land.

As you stand in ME
You will declare and decree My Will
And watch it come to pass.
As Moses parted the Red Sea
So will My Voice, spoken through you,
Move mountains in the spiritual realm.

Battle lines have been drawn
My Army awaits My command
You, Mighty Soldier, have been chosen
For this day, this hour
Stand strong … lift up your eyes toward Heaven
Take your position … be alert
Your Sword, the Word of God
Will tear down strongholds and defeat the enemy
VICTORY has already been won by the Blood of My Son …
JESUS!

A GREAT AWAKENING

"A great awakening is coming," declares the Lord
"Fires have purified the body
She is now prepared to step into My Fullness.
So awaken My children and see!
Look around … My fires are springing up
Don't you see? Don't you feel My presence?

The bowl has tipped over
Thunder, lightning, wind, and rain fill the atmosphere
Until every soul is awakened to My Power and My Glory!
A shaking has revealed the hidden evil, the hidden darkness
Righteous judgments now bring TRUTH!
Watch My sons and daughters take their positions.

Demons tremble before My Chosen Ones,
As lost souls are snatched out of Satan's hands.
My army, fully clothed with Heaven's armor,
Takes back territory from every demonic stronghold across this land.
The ground shakes, and mountains fall
As Holy Victory is echoed around the world,
RIGHTEOUSNESS STANDS! RIGHTEOUSNESS STANDS!"

A New Era

In the midst of all the chaos in this world
Jehovah is still on the throne
His righteousness is still the plumb line
That divides truth from deception
His Word still stands as the measuring rod
That separates holiness from evil
Power still radiates from the Holy Spirit
Bringing life to each seed of salvation
A new era is unfolding
Peeling away layers and layers of
Satanic deception
With the breath of the Holy Spirit
Life takes flight
It soars above waves of destruction
Depositing seeds of hope, peace, and love

A sound reverberates across the land,
"Eye has not seen nor has ear heard
The glorious sound of deliverance
That touches every man, woman, and child!
Behold the soon returning Kind of Kings
STANDS ready to pierce the sky!"

The Highway of Our GOD

Make straight the highway of our GOD
No turning, eyes straight ahead
For tomorrow is today, and today is tomorrow.

Every stumbling stone will be removed
As the LORD of Hosts marches forward
Kings bow down; leaders fall on their faces
As GOD's Shekinah Glory hovers over the nations.

Righteousness rules again
Evil and darkness try to hide
But El Shaddai, The Almighty GOD, sees ALL
Look up … see the Lion of the Tribe of Judah ROAR

Every high place will be brought low
Every low place will be raised up
For the soon returning King of Kings

Righteousness will be the cornerstone
On which man's actions will be judged
PREPARE … PREPARE …
For hearts will be laid bare
Before the coming of the Great I AM.

Rise Up

Rise up oh mighty warrior of God
Stand strong … begin to declare My Will.
The enemy cannot stand against the power of My Word.

Holy Spirit come
Fill My child with wisdom and knowledge
Let the authority that comes from the Great I AM
Guide, direct, and empower you.
See into the spiritual realm.
Demons fall as My Word is proclaimed
No evil entity can succeed against Adonai ELOHIM
Every knee must bow before ME!

Watch the Lion of the tribe of Judah roar
Open Wide your mouth
Decree a thing and it shall be accomplished.
I have called you to be My Light, to stand in the gap, and to declare My Truth.

Stand Strong … do NOT fear
Greater is the One in you then he that roams in the darkness.
Watch My Sword destroy everything that exalts itself above Yeshua
Stand Strong Mighty Warrior
STAND STRONG!

Waiting

Search my heart, oh Lord,
Cleanse me with hyssop
Purify my inner man
Until there is nothing left but You.

Teach me to wait and listen
Let Your Spirit mold me into a vessel
Worthy of honorable use.

A war wages inside my soul
Wanting to move but hearing that still small voice say,
"Wait!"
Quietness settles over me
As the Hand of God purifies and makes ready.

When, Lord, when?
Suddenly, anointing oil from Heaven
Begins to flood and consume me
Love more powerful than anything one could think or imagine
Saturates my inner man until ...
All that is left is pure LIGHT!

Reach Out

My people die for lack of knowledge
Won't you go across this land
Teaching and demonstrating My Truth?

Lead by example
Let Me use your hands and feet
Saturate your soul with My Words
Allow the Spirit to show you the way.

I don't need excellent speech
Just a surrendered heart filled with My Love
Reach out with a helping hand and a loving touch.

Show the lost My Goodness
The world needs to see Me in you
Spend time with Me and I will direct your steps.

I am calling you back to Me
Cast aside your desires and seek My face
Allow Me to change you into My image of Holiness.

Put on Your Armor

Awake sleeper, there is work to be done
So arise, put on your armor … take the sword, the Word of God!
The mist is parting and the LIGHT is beginning to shine
Look about … do you see the Heavenly Host
Standing at attention, waiting for the command?

Where is the commander?
Why it is you, the one seated in heavenly places
Listening to the Holy Spirit, waiting for the Word to be released
SUDDENLY, the command comes forth
"Declare, Declare, Declare … Call for the army of God, GO!"
Strategies and assignments are given out
To those fully equipped to wage war.

Standing alongside the Heavenly Host, God's children
march side by side in unity
Explosions shatter enemy strongholds, exposing
the demonic beneath
With the Dumas power of God, Light arises over the
Lord's chosen ones.

As they step out from the Presence of Yahweh
Prepared to take back territory stolen by the evil one,
A hush falls across the land, as God's mighty sons and daughters
Begin to Speak and Declare.

Wave after wave of the WORD pierces the Earth's atmosphere
Mountains quake and the heavens shake as the Glory of the Lord
Resounds across the airways, breaking the power of the enemy
Not by might, not by sword … but by the SPOKEN WORD of GOD
Redemption and freedom sing loudly announcing the Greatness and
Majesty of
YAHWEH!

A New Day

A new day … a new day has dawned
The old is gone … new seeds have sprouted
A fresh wind is blowing across towns and cities
Separating wheat from chaff and purifying the soil for rebirth.

Out of the ashes, life and hope emerge
Unified prayer has prepared the soil
Water from the Word of God saturates the ground
Giving life to seedlings.
Watch as the oil flows, saturating each new plant
An acceleration of growth causes each one to soar
Until meadows are covered in a vibrant array of colors.

The Son pours His love on each flower
Until its branches touch the heavens
Who are these new plants that are filled with such beauty?
Why they are God's chosen ones
They have emerged out of chaos, reborn in the likeness of their Father
Radiant with the pure love of Yahweh!

They move in unity as One
Filling the earth with a new holiness and righteousness
That turns darkness into pure LIGHT!

Proclaim

Proclaim, proclaim My Truth
For it shall proceed out of your mouth
Turning dead things to life.

No turning back
Once Truth is declared,
All will be judged according to My Word.

No longer will man seek but not find.
My truth shall reverberate across this land
Saturating every son and daughter.

Then shall they understand …
After that, shall they make a decision
To believe and turn
Or to follow the path of the enemy.

Lies will be exposed
As My Word covers this earth.
Only then can man choose wisely.
Which Truth will you follow -
The living Word of God or the deceptions of the enemy?
Chose LIFE!

The Calling

The Lord reigns and rules over all the earth
His righteousness endures forever
He rests His hand upon those who fear Him
Anointing His servants with power from on high
His children go forth proclaiming the wonders of the Almighty
Raising the dead, healing the sick
Casting out each demon that interferes with the Master's plan

Nothing, no nothing can stand when the Greatness on High speaks
For He seeks those who are hungry
Those who are searching
Those who harken to His call

Are you ready? Have you heard?
That still small voice speaks
Listen...Listen... the Master calls
Step out; step in as the anointing flows
Cloth yourself with the Spirit
Go, do as He commands

Spread the Word, share the gifts
For the time is short
The Lord wants none to parish
GO... DO... as He commands!

United as One

The righteous will stand in the midst of trouble
Their eyes looking up at the Great I AM
Surrounded by God's mighty army, they watch and listen
Shalom, peace, covers each son and daughter
Fear has no power over the Lord's holy ones because …
They have found wisdom and truth
The All Knowing … the All Seeing protects His own.

What can mere man do to God's servants?
These earthly warriors know who they are in Christ
These earthly warriors know Yeshua has fully equipped them
To subdue nations, to bind demons, to smash the very gates of Hell.

As this new season rises out of the dust of the old
Sanctified men and women STAND …
Reaching higher to become and to be
Nature itself senses a change, as this new day dawns
Bowing low, creation acknowledges that the Lord's children
Are now redeemed and purified,
Walking in the authority of their Creator
Bringing God's Will to this earthly atmosphere
Purity, holiness, and obedience rain down
As the oil of the Spirit saturates each child
Uniting them as ONE consecrated body!

The Soon Returning King

Are you ready My child?
For the King is mounting
Preparing for battle.
Are you ready to meet the Lord?

Lean not unto your own understanding
Lean on the Word
Stand on the Word
Battle with the Word

For the Word rises up
Sword in hand
Slicing back and forth, back and forth,
Separating truth from sin
Wisdom from folly

Every knee will bow
At the appearance of the King
Watch, be alert
Listen … do you hear it?

The sound of the shofar
Announcing the coming of the King of Kings
Some fall on their faces crying
"Cover me, rocks. Hide me."
Others stand, looking up
Hands raised in adoration
Which one are you, my child?
Are you ready?

A Unified Bride

As the days lengthen
And spring peeps over the horizon,
So does the Lord's mercy and love.
His purifying fire has sharpened His bride
For the days ahead and the battles yet to be won.

Emerging out of the grave of apathy
Rises a unified body of believers with power
and purpose
This new army knows its calling and its assignment.

As the shofar is sounded and
thanksgiving and
praise fill the atmosphere,
The ground begins to SHAKE!
Can you hear it? Can you feel it?
This new army of the Great I AM
Stands together as ONE ... eyes
straight ahead
Waiting for the command to move out.
They never break rank but move in unity
Fear is under their feet and victory is their cry.

Be ready and be prepared!
For the final days are here
The Lion of the Tribe of Judah reigns supreme!

Prayer Prayer Prayer

Prayer Prayer Prayer
Nothing is birthed without prayer,
Cracks in the enemy's foundation
Expand as prayers go up.

Walls begin to collapse
As intercessors declare and decree
God's Holy Word.

Joining with the Angelic Army
God's mighty sons and daughters
Move in the supernatural.
Strongholds come crashing down
Lies and deceptions are exposed
As the angelic and the Bride
Move in unity and strength.

Prayer Prayer Prayer
The Lord is calling His Chosen Ones back
To a sacrificial life of prayer.

"For My thoughts are not your thoughts
Neither are your ways My ways,
Declares the Lord"

Isaiah 55:8 AMPC

My child, even though you do not understand
Believe … Faith means unshakeable trust.
I am the Author and Finisher of all life
My purpose and plan generate My perfect Will in this earthly realm.

There is a constant spiritual battle between
Light and darkness, goodness and evil, truth and deception
Allow My Spirit to do His work in you,
For I have chosen you to be My voice in this latter day
As you stand in the gap and declare My Word …
A quaking and shaking begin … hear the roar intensify
Strongholds collapse; demons tremble; satanic fortresses lie in ruins.

My Righteousness shall be established
As My sons and daughters pray and decree My Word.
Have you been called? Have you been appointed?
Arise, My loved ones and look …
Around the world My elect take their positions
Prepared for battle with the Sword of the Spirit, they move in unity
Bringing I AM's Will to completion.
ARISE, Mighty Army of God, ARISE!

The Time is Now

Stir the fire … stir the fire
Oh Holy One of Israel … stir the fire
The earth is ready for a move of God
Prepare hearts; open closed minds
Holy Spirit come and sweep across this land.

"You are in a season of dedication to My perfect Will," declares the Lord.
"Allow My Spirit to purify, to cleanse, to saturate
The harvest is ripe, but where are the reapers?

My Presence will always go with you
As you move to bring in the lost
No weapon formed against you shall prosper
Because I AM is always your rear guard
Never fear, My little one, for you have My anointing, My power.

Look across the fields and see those that are seeking Truth
Come … reap the harvest
Bring in the hurting, the disillusioned, the deceived
My anointing rests on you … go forth in the power of the Most High
I have called you for this season … no turning back, no turning back!"

LIFT UP YOUR EYES

As days grow darker, lift up your eyes
See the ONE standing at the gate
Ready and prepared to move!

He is calling His chosen ones to rise up
"I have given you the keys to the Kingdom
Move in the authority I have entrusted to you
Stand in the gap and declare and decree My Word.

In My Name bind every demonic entity
Whatever you bind is already bound in Heaven
The enemy must bow before Me
He has no authority in this earthly realm
Unless My children cower in fear before him.

I stripped him of all power at the cross
So move out and deliver those held captive
Restore justice and peace through the spoken Word of God
Rise up, My sons and daughters … Stand Strong!
Sound the alarm and declare My Righteousness!
For I will strengthen you with My Righteous Right Hand!

The VICTORY has already been WON!"

ARISE

ARISE, Army of GOD, ARISE!
The seed birthed in you is BREAKING forth!
No more will man say, "Where is this GOD of yours?"
For they will see and comprehend
The True GOD, the GREAT I AM, rules this world!

Tongues will be silent,
As the Glory of the LORD hovers over the earth.
Brought to their knees
The sons of men will confess their sins,
Causing a shaking in the regions of darkness.

Light breaks forth
Sending wave after wave of GOD's redemptive power …
Strongholds come crashing down
As barriers are carried away by the LORD's Angelic Hosts.

A NEW DAY has dawned
As GOD's chosen, GOD's elect, stand in His Power
Releasing the Anointing of the SPIRIT
The LORD, ADONAI – Tzva'ot, the LORD of Heaven's armies,
Stands at the gate calling,
"COME!"

The Whisper of the Spirit

The sweet whisper of the Spirit
Calling me back into His Presence
Where life originates, and visions and dreams are restored.

There in the loving arms of the Father, transformation begins
What now Lord? What do you desire from me?

"Only you, child, only you
Come home, My little one, come home
Run into your Daddy's arms where peace and hope are found.

I have much I want to give you
But the enemy has asked to sift you
Have you opened doors, allowing the evil one to enter?
Turn quickly and repent …
Then and only then will the enemy have no legal access
Sin separates, but repentance purifies.

Quiet yourself, listen, and heed that still small voice,
Come, return … forgiveness awaits."

PEACE

Shalom, Peace, is a river that floods our souls
Just as water overwhelms the ground
So does our Father's Peace seep into every pore of our being
"My Peace," says the Lord, "is not like the world's
It is everlasting for those who choose to follow Me
Many hear the evil one's voice and follow his path,
But My sons and daughters know My voice and
choose to listen.
As My Words saturate their spirit man, so does My Peace.

A calm, gentle wind surrounds each child
Infusing wisdom, knowledge, and wholeness into My creation
My Name, Yahweh Shalom, rests on My chosen ones
When storms rage, My Peace stills their souls
Others cry out in fear and anger
But My anointed ones stand and battle
Never looking back, they move toward the Light
Becoming a beacon of hope for the lost and dying!"

<u>Shalom:</u> peace, tranquility, safety, well-being, welfare,
health, contentment, success, comfort, wholeness, integrity
Thank You Father for Your Peace!

Hear, Oh Israel

Hear, oh Israel, the Lord thy God is ONE!
Hear, oh nations of the world, the Lord thy God is ONE!
Hear, oh peoples of this earth, the Lord thy God is ONE!
There is no other god but the Great I AM!

Every tongue, every nation, every people will bow before Me
None can save; none can deliver; none can set free, but Yahweh
Bow down … humble yourself before Me
Let My mighty hand mold you
Allow My Spirit to do His work in you.

Then and only then will you be ready for the Master's use.
You have many idols, many gods in your life
Search your hearts … what have you placed above me?
Cleanse yourself … remove ALL that stands above the Great I AM!

As the Spirit moves to reveal Truth to you
Fall on your face, repent, and turn
Then My dunamis power will rest on you
Moving mountains and anything else that lifts itself above Me!!
Arise now, My children,
Once cleansed, move out into position
Take back all that has been stolen; rebuild the walls and the gates
STAND in the gap for the lost
I AM has spoken!

The Roar of My People

Hear the roar of My people
"Save us, deliver us!"
Where is My army of believers?
Have you forsaken your post?
Why have your eyes been blinded?
Your ears closed to the Holy Spirit.
Don't you hear Me calling you out of darkness
To be My light, My refuge to My sons and daughters?

Rise up! Stand on your feet
Plant them firmly on the ROCK
Heed My Voice … walk in obedience
Be fully equipped for battle
Don't bow down … don't fear
For I have called you to deliver your brothers and sisters around the world.

When you speak … I Speak
When you declare … I Declare
When you move … I Move
Look up and see My Mighty Army that surrounds you … preparing the way
Move out and take back every child held in the grip of Satan
For victory has already been achieved by the Blood of My Son
JESUS!

Prayer for Alignment

Align my heart with Your Heart, oh Lord
My words with Your Word
My spirit with You, Holy Spirit.

For Holy alignment brings about Your Will
It brings redemption, restoration, power, wisdom, and peace
So have Your way, Father, in me.

When I am one with You
No weapon formed against me shall stand
When my words align with Your Will, dunamis power flows out.

Saturate me, Lord, with Your anointing
Open new doors that bring Your righteousness
For Your plans are not my plans
Your ways are higher than I can comprehend.

As I move into this new position
Prepare my inner man for Your perfect will
Guide my footsteps into unknown territories
Everywhere my feet touch will be Yours
Strengthen me, Father, and seal me with Your Spirit
Then I can move in and through You
Let Your Light radiate into the darkest regions
Bringing hope and peace with every step You and I take
For You, Daddy, deserve ALL the HONOR and GLORY.
Amen, so be it.

WATCH AND WAIT

Watch and wait!
Just as Elijah's servant
Saw a small cloud rising from the sea
Before the barrage of rain began to fall,
So shall you stand at your post
And see a cloud of righteousness
Forming across this land.
Evil spirits tremble in fear
As the cloud grows in power and purpose,
Declaring holy judgements upon all.

Suddenly, lightning flashes across the sky
As God's Word bursts forth
Breaking every lie, every demonic deception
Piercing even the depths of Hell.
Then Truth rises out of the ashes
As men and women of darkness fall to the ground.
For only those covered by the blood of the Lamb
Can stand before a Holy God.

LIGHT _____ DARKNESS
Where do you stand?

Holy God

Oh Holy, Righteous God
You stand and watch
Searching for the intercessors who are the watchmen
Will You find any?

"Yes," declares the Lord, "I have a remnant that is holy
They have exchanged their dirty, stained clothes
For My garments that have been washed in the blood of the Lamb
They have been found worthy and righteous because they believe."

"A time is coming," says the Lord, "when the storms will escalate
As deep darkness seems to cover the land
However, My Light will shine brighter as My righteous ones unite
Filled with the oil and new wine, they will move with power and authority
Penetrating the very gates of Hell."

Nations will tremble as the shofar announces a new wave of holiness
A purging and purifying will settle over the earth
Are you clothes clean? Have you been redeemed by the blood?
The Master is calling His servants to a lifestyle of righteousness,
faithfulness, and obedience
"Then and only then will your prayers be heard," declares the Lord.

Peace Be Still

Peace, be still, My little ones
No one knows the hour or the day
But the promised coming
Of your King draws near.
You must prepare the way.
Move in My Anointing
Let My Spirit guide and direct you
Snatch those dying out of the fire.

My Light in each child will draw the lost
So let your light shine in the darkness.
Be prepared with My message
Of repentance, hope, and life.

As you infiltrate the enemy's territory,
Let the oil of My Presence exude out of you
Breach the walls of resistance
With the Sword of My Spirit, the Word
Prepare … Prepare …
I will return for the Bride of Christ
The wedding supper is almost complete
So look up, be still, and listen for the sound of My Shofar
Calling My sons and daughters home!

Awake My Loved Ones

Awake My loves ones

Don't you see … don't you know?

Righteousness and holiness are under the feet of tolerance.

Blind eyes open!

Deaf ears hear!

My Word is TRUTH

I AM does not change

I AM is the same yesterday, today, and forever!

Look about and weep

Scales have covered your vision

How you ask? … Little by little, inch by inch

The serpent has slowly slithered into My House

Camouflaged as love, this evil serpent has twisted and turned

The TRUTH of My Word into a lie!

So rise up, body of Christ

Cast out any doctrine or belief that goes against My Holy Word

Purify, deliver, and set free!

My House will be a House of Prayer, Praise, Fire, and Power

My remnant will rise and become the light that changes cities,

nations, and the world!

Behold the LAMB

Behold the LAMB comes
Bringing healing and deliverance
Sealing the sons and daughters
With the Power of the Holy Spirit

Arise … Look up …
See the SON coming on the clouds
Measuring out justice for all
No more will the enemy have victory
The curse is broken by the Blood

That pure, spotless Blood of the LAMB
Poured out for all who will receive
RUN to the Throne of Grace
Time is short

Are you ready to stand before the Lord?
All is exposed to the Truth of the Word
Set your hearts free
Receive the Perfect Love
That was poured out for you
COME … RECEIVE …
The free gift of LIFE
JESUS

Orange ~ Warfare, Fire of God

PART THREE

Warnings

"But if the watchman sees the sword coming and does not blow the trumpet and the people are not warned, and the sword comes and takes any one of them, he is taken away in and for his perversity and iniquity, but his blood will I require at the watchman's hand."

Ezekiel 33:6 AMPC

"Son of man, I have made you a watchman for the house of Israel; therefore hear a word from My mouth, and give them warning from Me: 18When I say to the wicked, 'You shall surely die,' and you give him no warning, nor speak to warn the wicked from his wicked way, to save his life, that same wicked man shall die in his iniquity; but his blood I will require at your hand. 19Yet, if you warn the wicked, and he does not turn from his wickedness, nor from his wicked way, he shall die in his iniquity; but you have delivered your soul.

Ezekiel 3:17-19 NKJV

CRY AND WEEP!

Cry and weep, body of Christ, cry and weep
For the sins of complacency and apathy
That has gripped the church!
Where is the sorrow, the deep, repentant sorrow,
For the idols and self-serving pleasures
That occupy and consume your thoughts?

Rather than mourning over the dead fetuses
And the children left to the schemes of the evil one,
We sit in our homes as contented sons and daughters
Focusing on our own passions rather than seeking our Father's heart.

Wail and cry out for the lost souls the enemy has captured
Don't you understand that demons have no power
Unless we surrender the authority that was purchased for us at the cross!

Rise up … fast, repent, and pray
God is sifting the chaff from the wheat
Where do you stand … obedience or rebellion?
Tough words … tough choices
Search your hearts and ask of the Spirit
TRUTH

Truth

Beware My little ones
My Word is Truth
From beginning to end
Not one Word will fall to the ground
Open your blinded eyes
Ask for My healing salve
To restore your sight
Into the Truth of My Holy Word

Blind eyes … Be Opened
Deaf ears … Hear My Truth
Be transformed into the child
I have created you to be

Sound the alarm
Throughout the earth
Come and repent
For the Great I AM
Stands knocking on your door
Heed My Voice
Come to the Throne of Mercy while there is time
RUN into My open arms
Where rest and peace will shelter you … COME QUICKLY

CONSUMED

Consumed … Consumed
Where did the time go?
What had God planned for me that did not get completed?
Lord, why was I distracted?
Why was I carried away with activities that have no heavenly value?
Can I redeem the time?

My child listen; time is short
The enemy delights in deception, in deceiving each son and daughter
Bringing an end before My plan begins.
Beware of the enemy's strategy to strip away minutes, hours, days
Until nothing is left; nothing is accomplished
Ask of Me pure wisdom and discernment
Ask of Me direction and purpose

For My ways are higher

My plans bring My desires forth

My Will shall stand whether My children obey or not.

Keep your ears close to My lips

Focus your eyes on My Word

Listen to the direction of the Holy Spirit

Go and do ALL I have prepared for you

Don't be slack … I am with you always!

Listen ... Obey

Listen and obey
That is all I ask
Seek My face not My hand
Believe in Jehovah ... never doubt.
Look up ... look out
See the stars too numerous to count
There is nothing impossible for El Shaddai.

As of old ...
Words spoken by the anointing of the Spirit
Caused My alignment and My purpose
To move into position.
Suddenly, a shaking began
In the deepest region of Sheol
Demons quaked in fear
As My Word echoed across the earth.

Light shined in the darkness
Chains tumbled to the ground
Salvation was birthed
At the cross on Golgotha
So ARISE Mighty Warriors of GOD
Declare and Decree My Word
And it shall come to pass ... Just LISTEN and OBEY!

Crucify My Flesh

Send down Your Holy Fire, Lord,
To purify Your children
To cleanse and make holy Your own.
Consume everything that stands in the way of total submission.

Father, once submitted, let the washing of Your Word
Transform each child into the one
He or she was created to be.
Fill Your children with every good and perfect gift
That emanates from Your Presence.
Once cleansed and filled, Lord, breathe new life into
each son and daughter.

Send out this rebirthed army
To conquer and dismantle every Satanic stronghold and weaponry
That has corrupted and held bound nations, peoples,
and generations.
Fully equipped, these men and women, chosen by
the Great I AM,
Will deliver, set free, and restore
Those who were chained, bound, and deceived.

Then will these lost sons and daughters raise their hands
to a Holy God
In praise and adoration.
For the work only a Savior on a cross could complete.
JESUS is the Way, the Truth, and the Life!

GRIEVED

My chosen ones
My Spirit is grieved
Over sin and disobedience
I have a purpose and plan for each child
But it cannot be birthed
Until My sons and daughters diligently seek My Face.

Wondrous things that can't be imagined
Are in store for each child,
But obedience and sacrifice are required for the manifestation of
My Presence
To move mountains and bring forth My Will and My blessings.

Be My voice in this generation
Be My hands and feet
I have given you everything you need
But only those who walk in holiness will move in the supernatural
Only those who have an unwavering spirit will walk in
My footsteps.

There is no greater love than to lay down one's life for another
Daily place your wants, your desires at the foot of the cross
Test Me now in this ... see the proof of My Word echo across this land
As My chosen ones align their will with MINE.
2 Peter 1:5-8

Burn, Destroy, Rebuild

If eyes could see and ears could hear
Would Your children still doubt, Lord,
That You are God and Your Word is TRUTH?

Lord, have mercy and stir the fire
Let the flames consume
All that does not line up with Your Word!

Burn, destroy, and then rebuild
From the foundation up
Let every level be rooted in the blood of Jesus!

No bends, no weaknesses, but layer upon layer
Of the Word of God until …
Every thought, every action is sealed
Now justice and righteousness join together
To establish Your Holiness upon this earth!

ARE YOU READY

A voice calling in the wilderness,
"Prepare the way of the LORD."
Are you ready?
Are you planted in good soil?
Are you walking in obedience?
Soon, very soon, we will stand before the Law Giver
To give an account of our earthly life.

What shall we say when we stand before our King
When His Light shines into the deepest part of our souls
Exposing every hidden thought …
Every hidden action … every hidden sin?
Are they covered by the Blood of the Lamb?

"Return" … "Come home" … the Savior calls
Set your house in order
The day or the hour … no one knows
But look up … see the King of Kings with His Mighty Warriors
Prepared for battle … coming for His chosen ones
But destroying all His enemies
"Which one are you?" the still, small voice whispers.
"Which one are you?"

WAR CRY

Hear My cry
My War Cry intensifies across the planet
Don't look back
Keep your eyes straight ahead

The battle has begun
There's no turning back
Only the righteous … the holy
Will hear and heed My Voice

Prepare … Prepare
Are you walking in purity … in holiness?
Are your words and actions lining up with My Word?
Let go of any hindrance
Rip off all entanglements

Clothe yourself with the full armor of God
Plant your feet firmly on the ROCK
Don't cower … Stand strong
As the Purifying Wind of My Spirit thunders across this land
Every hidden sin will be exposed and uncovered
Only the RIGHTEOUS will remain STANDING

THE SWORD

As the lion has no mercy
Upon its prey,
So shall My Sword, My Word,
Upon the demonic.

Dare to believe; dare to stand
My Word is My Power
That manifests in this earthly realm.
Put on My complete armor
Pick up your sword
Slash back and forth
demolishing
all the lies of the enemy.
My Power has been
entrusted to you

Prepare your heart to receive and obey
Wait upon the Spirit for wisdom
Only in Me will you be victorious.

I have given you everything you need.
Go forth now and conquer
Retrieve that which has been lost or stolen
Pick up your Sword and move into position.
Might and power are in your hands
Be bold, be courageous
Don't fear because I AM is with you
Victory has already been won
At the Cross.

Righteousness

"Right standing with Me is what I require
Not man … not friends … not family
Stand before a Holy God with an open heart
All obedience … all love … all loyalty
Then I can use you
Then I can mold you into My image
Then you are ready for My service.

There is no other way
You must decide … Me or self?
My heart yearns for My bride
To come boldly before the throne
Hands lifted high in praise and adoration.

Spirit to spirit is My desire
Sit awhile and soak in My Presence
Allow Me to fill and refill you daily
There is much I want to impart to you
But you must come humbly and receive."

I AM is calling His chosen ones
To a place of intimacy
Where true freedom reigns
And lives are forever changed!

WARNING

Warning, Warning, Warning
Beware the tactics of the enemy
A wolf in sheep's clothing
Appears to be humble and obedient
But underneath are dead man's bones.

True humility, true obedience
Is the Light that burns in the darkness

Traps and snares are planted by the evil one
Only through the eyes of the Spirit
Can the body see and understand the schemes
of the demonic

Awake sleeping giant
Repent, Repent, Repent
Judgment is coming
Be ready, be prepared
Watch, warn, sound the alarm
Only by the Blood can one be saved
Only by the Blood can one be delivered
Only by the BLOOD of JESUS

MY WORD

Search Me; search My Word

I AM does not lie

If I said it, will I not perform it?

My prophets have declared My Will, both to bless and to punish.

If I, Yahweh, am the same yesterday, today, and forever;

Will not My plan and purpose succeed!

There are no other gods that know the end from the beginning

Watch the fulfillment of My Word come to pass.

Are you faithful … are you steadfast?

Do you walk in obedience, seeking My face and heart each day?

My sons and daughters know My voice

They listen and heed My direction

When the enemy rises up to destroy, My children stand in the gap and intercede.

My Power rests upon My servants

The evil one trembles in their presence because he knows his time is short.

Be ready, My little ones …

Greater is He that is within you

Then he who is in the world.

Stand Strong … put on My complete armor

The battle has begun

STAND STRONG!

THE LION AND THE LAMB

Every man, woman, and child
Will stand before a Holy God
Which one will you meet first?

The LAMB

A gentle nudging, a still, small voice,
Calling, urging, whispering,
"Come home, child … I love you!"
Your Daddy's arms open wide
Inviting you to step inside, where love, peace, and refuge are found.
Covered with the wings of grace, each son and daughter finds rest.

The LION

Mighty, powerful, omnipotent
Eyes that expose all darkness, all sin
Shine into the depths of man's soul
What will the Lion of Judah see?
The blood of the Lamb or the iniquity that destroys and kills
There is no turning back
When the Book of Life is opened, will your name be found?
Enter through the narrow gate … how you ask?

Jesus is the only way

By no other name can one be saved
He is the Alpha and Omega, the Beginning and the End
Choose the LAMB while there is still time!

The Call

The call of repentance is heard throughout the land
Fall on your knees and cry out to the ONE Who can save you
Search your hearts … what is first in your life?
No turning back … no turning back
Yahweh alone can save
Yahweh alone can bring peace
Yahweh alone can deliver and set free.

Has the oil in your lampstand grown dim?
Does your light beckon others to follow?
Ask of the Lord pure oil
Cry out for more holiness, more anointing
Weep for the lost, the hurting, the deceived
Grieve over the sins that consume so many
Change course … change direction
Seek the Master's face not His hand … plead for mercy
Wail and lament over the sin in the body of Christ
Ask of the Lord wisdom and discernment
Ask of the Lord fire … fire to consume wickedness and cleanse
and sanctify each child
Then and only then can the Lord's army of believers rise.

Once purified, a noise is heard around the world
A roar so intense that demons shutter in fear
What's that sound … it is the Army of the Most Holy God
Moving in unity and destroying every demonic stronghold
Shouts of praise and adoration fill the atmosphere
As lost souls are set free, and the strongman is bound!

The Battle Begins

The sound of the Shofar summons
Come to the feast of the Lord
Angelic Hosts stand guard
Harkening to the Voice of our God

Move into position
Ready your sword
Put on the breastplate of righteousness
Focus your heart on His calling
Now is the time to move
Watch, can you perceive it?
A mighty army of believers seizing the horns of the altar
Declaring and decreeing the release of captives

Demons shutter in fear
Strongholds come thundering down
Feel LIBERTY
As the captives are released

Wave after wave, the Anointing encircles the Earth
No place to hide
All exposed to the eyes of the Lord
Battle lines are drawn
The Church ascends to take its position
Preparing a home for the lost
Setting a place at the table of our God
Victory, celebration, praise
Lost souls find their shelter in the Arms of the *SAVIOR*

Are You Prepared

Arise, man and woman of God, Arise
Step into position that was created just for you
Shift from the old into the new
Mount up for I have called you ... Mount up

Begin to see this earthly domain through My eyes
You have been commissioned by Yahweh
To stand in My authority
To decree My Word
To bind the spirits of darkness
To deliver and set free those held bound
To bring My Will into this earthly realm

So STAND and fight using My weapons of war
You have been entrusted with the keys of the Kingdom
When much is given ... much is required
Are you ready? Are you prepared?
There is no turning back
Victory demands sacrifice and obedience
Count the cost ... submission is mandatory
"Are you ready? Are you prepared" asked the Lord.

The ROAR

Listen … be still

Can you hear it?

The roar grows Louder and LOUDER

Crashing into the very portals of Hell

The ROAR of the Lion of the Tribe of Judah

Covers every region of this world

SUDDENLY … barricades come down

Chains dissolve into rubble as the ROAR intensifies!

Look … who stands beside the Lion?

It's the Mighty Warriors of the Lord of Host

Moving across this land, destroying anything that stands in the way of our victorious KING!

Kings and kingdoms must bow

Principalities, powers, and lords of this age must bow

Spiritual wickedness in heavenly places falls on its knees and begs for mercy.

For the Omnipotent, the Omniscient, the Omnipresent Yahweh reigns!

Forever and ever His Word shall stand

Most Holy is our God

Salvation and Power belong to Him

For He yields NOT His Glory to another!

THE AWAKENING AND THE CALLING OF THE HOLY SPIRIT ~ 77

Shake Us

Shake us, Lord, realign us,
Remove anything that stands in the way of Your perfect plan
Expose the strategy of the enemy
That tries to stop or hinder Your will for each life.

Search our hearts; convict us of sin
Of things that consume or squander our time
Purify and sanctify each son and daughter
The enemy has no power to kill, steal, or destroy
Unless, we the body, open the door.

Rise up, My child, the fire has been stirred
Assignments have been given ... will you receive and obey?
The earth groans and laments; mountains quake and rocks cry out
Waiting for God's Holy Army to arise ... will you heed the call?

Fear destroys, but faith sustains
Pride kills, but humility brings wisdom and honor
Choose this day whom you will serve ...
Choose LIFE so you may live
Choose JESUS!

REBUILD THE WALLS

Riots in the streets … confusion in the air
Sheep without a shepherd … wolves ready to devour
Why, Lord why?

"The gates are down … where are the intercessors?
Where are My warriors declaring My Word?
My call has gone forth, 'Rebuild the walls
Stand in the gap … call for repentance
Sharpen your swords … prepare, prepare, prepare!'

Align your sight with My Spirit
Allow Me to mold you and equip you
Fill you with insight, with discernment, with power
Are you willing to be reconciled to My Will,
Or are you stiff-necked and rebellious?
The walls cannot be rebuilt until My children humble themselves
Cast aside their own plans and desires
And place Me first in their lives.

No longer can you have divided loyalties
Your ways are not My ways … so turn
Then I can restore you and perform a perfect work
Then can you stand in the gap and rebuild the walls
Then and only then can the sheep hear the Truth, be set free, and LIVE!"

A Mighty Rushing Wind

A mighty rushing wind sweeps across the earth
Uprooting and tearing down strongholds
Purging and purifying every blood-bought child of the King.

Naked and bare, each son and daughter
Stands before a Holy God
All is exposed before the Truth of His Light
Lies and deceit that were once hidden
Now are revealed!
A sound of cleansing begins to emerge
Sorrow, repentance, and healing fill the atmosphere.

Suddenly, dead bones come to life
Fully clothed with the armor of God,
This new army of believers STANDS.
Fear swells in the regions of darkness
Because the end time warriors of God have ascended.

Nothing, absolutely nothing, can stand before the Almighty
Yahweh's Word will come to pass!

"Victory is Mine," declares the LORD!

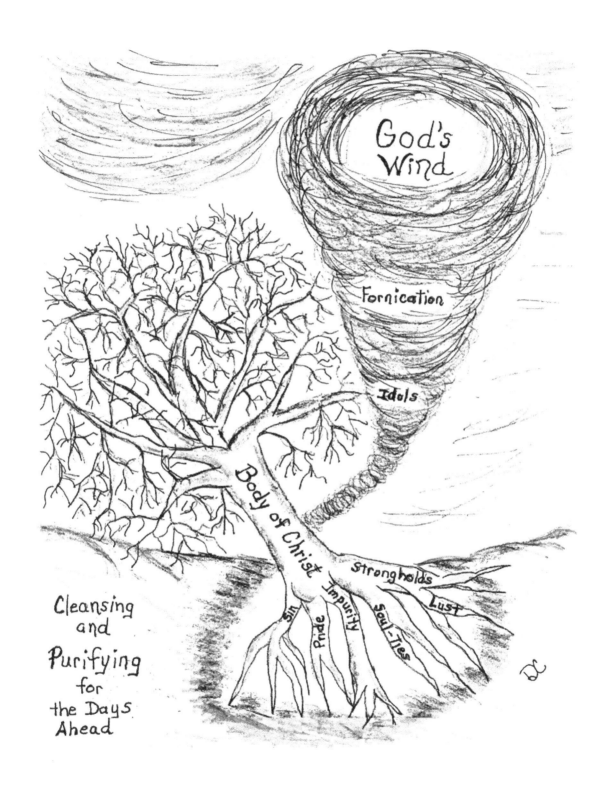

A Voice in the Wilderness

A voice crying in the wilderness
Prepare the way for our LORD
Wail and lament over sins and idols
Which have been planted above our Most Holy God.

Saturate the atmosphere with tears of sorrow and repentance.
Allow the Holy Spirit to use you as an intercessor
Stand in the gap.

It's not the lost who need to repent
They don't know and understand
But the body of Christ has allowed the evil one access to kill, steal, and destroy.
Sexual sins, greed, selfishness, jealousy, rebellion
Have opened the door for the demonic.

Cleanse your hearts and TURN
Heed that still small voice
Rise up and walk in the authority of ADONAI Tzva'ot, the Lord of Heaven's Army.
Put on the full armor that God provides

Get ready for battle
Don't give the enemy power
Disobedience is Satan's instrument to defeat the body of Christ.

Now is the time; now is the hour
Repent and TURN
Your Father's arms of LOVE and forgiveness await.

BEWARE

Beware … Beware … My child
Many false teachers, false prophets
Try to deceive the elect

Keep your eyes, your ears tuned to the Holy Spirit
Only He can give you Truth
Only He knows all things.

Flattering words tickle the ears
For evil is deceptive
Speaking lies … half truths

Beware My child
Only the great I AM knows the end from the beginning
Ask of Me pure wisdom … a discerning spirit
Ask of Me Truth.

For My plans will succeed
Be the watchman on the wall
See into the spiritual world
SOUND the alarm
For you have been called to guard the ANOINTING.
I will give you insight into hidden mysteries
Into the secret plans of the enemy
You will declare and decree a Word, and it shall be accomplished
Because My Righteous Right Hand is upon you
To bring My Will into this earthly realm.

Hear Ye, Hear Ye

Hear Oh America … Hear Oh Body of Christ
The Lord your God is One
Where are the repentant hearts?
Where are those who weep and mourn because of the idols that have been placed above the Great I AM?
Where are the intercessors, the gatekeepers,
the watchmen on the walls?

"You ask of Me peace, but there can be no peace until the walls and gates are rebuilt

You ask of Me wisdom and discernment, but your eyes and hearts
have turned away from My Word
You seek pleasure and gratification rather than My Face
Humble yourself ... fall on your knees and repent for your many idols,
Then turn back to Me
Set your eyes and ears to see and hear My Voice
Allow My Spirit to purify you
To mold you into the son or daughter I have created you to be.
Then and only then will I intervene and bring healing
to this land."
Holy, Holy, Holy are You, Lord
Righteous are Your judgements
You are TRUTH, and we bow in Your Presence
Let Your Glory rest upon Your servants!

> *"People who conceal their sins will not prosper,*
> *But if they confess and turn from them,*
> *they will receive mercy."*
>
> *Proverbs 28:13 NLT*

My child, you ask for much
Healing, gifts, prosperity, favor
But are you walking in holiness and righteousness?

Your sin will be exposed by the Truth of My Word
Repent and turn while there is still time
The days of My grace are numbered.

Where is your heart?
No more will My Spirit tolerate rebellion
This day decide whom you will serve
False idols or Adonai ELOHIM.

My Spirit searches the hearts and souls of mankind
Every unrepented sin separates you from My mercy
My Face has turned away
Because darkness can not dwell in My Presence.

Once more I will shake this earth
Repent, My child, and humble yourself
Then I, Adonai, will exalt you
And fill you with My joy, peace, and salvation!

OBEDIENCE

Obedience, obedience is all I desire
But how can you walk in obedience when you don't know Me?
Why are you seeking other idols,
When I AM stands before?

What idols you ask?
Those that steal your time; those that
consume your thoughts;
Those that bring Me no honor.

You say, "I love You, Lord!", but where are you?
How long since you have entered into My Presence?
How long since you have fed on My Word?
Words flow freely from your lips, but your actions
declare your true heart.

I desire to spend time with you, My child
Allow My Spirit to do His work
Wisdom, favor, power only come from submission
and sacrifice.

The enemy seeks to kill, steal, and destroy
But you have been called to be My Voice
So come, let My Fire do its work of cleansing, purifying, equipping
Arise, Stand, put on My armor and move into
position and listen
The sound of My Shofar Roars!

ONLY YAHWEH

A righteous son or daughter will fall, will fail
But will quickly repent and turn
Not so the unrighteous …

They fall, sin, and fail
But rather than repenting and turning
They set their faces like flint and continue on
Devising schemes and plots to go deeper into darkness

With eyes turned toward themselves
Only "I" matters
Hearts harden as time slips by, until all that is left is …
Greed, Pride, and Self

Only a merciful God can open blinded eyes
Only a merciful God loves the unlovable
Only a merciful God would send His SON
To be your sacrificial lamb
Only … YAHWEH

A Final Warning

In this new season, this new awakening
Plowing and planting will need greater determination
Focus and urgency will be keys.
In a blink, plowing will be closed
Planting will be completed
The fruit and the worker will stand side by side.

Souls are ready for this end time harvest
But will there be enough laborers
To bring in the bounty?
The Son is peaking over the clouds
Ready to rise in judgement and power
Once the Light begins to shine
Only those covered by the blood shall live.

Hurry, hurry, the call has gone out
Assignments are waiting … be prepared, be prepared!
Don't delay but listen and receive
Each one is given a number to bring home
Don't be slack or your souls will taste Hell!

STIR THE FIRE, LORD

"Are you ready? Are you ready for My fire?" asked the Lord.
"Yes, Lord, stir the fire!
Purify, cleanse, purge, refine
Separate the decayed from the pure
Let the Spirit open eyes to see the sin that lies within.
Once purified, Lord, mold each son and daughter into a vessel ready for the Master

Prepare hearts for an awakening and cultivate our fallow ground
Give single vision to Your chosen ones,
Eyes straight ahead, moving as ONE body."

Suddenly, an army emerges as God's Holy Vessels
No turning back ... No turning back!
A sound erupts, and God's Word is decreed
Strongholds tumble to the ground
Demons shriek with fear, for the resurrected church has taken its rightful position
Covered in the armor of God, the Lord's Mighty Ones stand victorious
Hand in hand with the Angelic Army, God's Word and Will are declared
Shock waves hit the very Gates of Hell,
Announcing there is only One who is Righteous!
The LION of the Tribe of Judah
The LORD JESUS CHRIST
YESHUA

Repent Repent Repent

Repent, repent, repent
Do you not perceive that a time of judgement
Is coming upon America if we, the body of Christ, do not repent.

Fall on your knees and cry out to God
Lament for the sins of our nation … for the sins of the church
Have you not heard …
"If My people who are called by My Name will humble themselves,
Pray, seek My face, and turn."
Stand in the gap and repent of our sins
Plead for mercy; not that we deserve it, but for the Lord's Name.
He created America for His Namesake to bring Him honor and glory.

Our Father is looking for someone to intercede on behalf of the nation
Will He find anyone?
Plead for the souls of the lost, for churches, for governments,
For the righteousness of Yeshua to be manifested throughout the land
Ask for forgiveness, mercy, revival.
Rise up, ye people of God … Stand and make up the hedge
Beseech the Lord for our nation
Then, "He will hear from Heaven and heal our land."

WHAT WILL PEOPLE SAY?

What will people say, what will people say
When time is up
Running to and fro
Right and left, left and right
Searching and looking for what?
The trumpet has sounded
All that remains is judgement.

Did you wait too long?
Didn't you hear the Master calling,
Tugging, pulling on your heart.

"Why, why didn't we respond?
We felt His loving touch,
We heard that still small voice,
Calling us home.
Lord, is it too late?
Can we still come home?
We'll be good; we'll work hard."

But the door has closed
Time has run out!
Can you hear the noise?
Wailing, weeping, and gnashing of teeth.

A soft whisper calls,
"The door is almost closed.
Hurry, hurry – come home My child."
The Master reaches forth His hand …
Will you take it?

WARNING! WARNING! WARNING!

Warning Warning Warning
Body of Christ arise!
The sound of the shofar blares
A battle cry is heard across the land.

Prepare Prepare Prepare
Stand guard ... move into position
The command has gone forth
Battle lines are drawn
Look up ... see the Host of Heaven
Arrayed in full armor, standing at attention.

Suddenly there is a violent shaking ...
As the Commander-in-Chief steps forth
A holy hush sweeps across the heavens
Waiting for the Word to be released!

Raising His arms, Yeshua proclaims,
"Father God, Yahweh, has declared
It is time to reap the harvest.
GO!"

BLUE ~ Holy Spirit, Word of God

PART FOUR

Holy Spirit's Lessons and Words

"But the Helper, the Holy Spirit, whom the
Father will send in My name,
He will teach you all things, and bring to your
remembrance all things that
I said to you."

John 14:26 NKJV

Every segment of this book was designed and directed by the Holy Spirit. Rather than a collection of poems, Part 4 is an assortment of words, thoughts, and teachings given to me by the unction of the Holy Spirit. Each lesson, which produced growth, maturity, and fruit, became a seed planted and rooted in my soul. I have learned that listening, receiving, and obeying are not always easy. Even though there have been some battle scars, every trial and every test was an opportunity to grow, overcome, and emerge victorious on the other side.

The greatest gift bestowed on each child of God is the gift of the Holy Spirit. He has been given to the Body to strengthen, encourage, comfort, teach, and convict. When He urges you to step out of your comfort zone and do something new and often times difficult, just know that He will be by your side. He will never leave you but will be your greatest helper, strength, and source. Never fear but look to the One who created you and loves you with a never ending love!

My first book, <u>My Journey with the Lord</u>, required total trust and dependency on the Holy Spirit. Daily, I had to seek direction and guidance from a loving Father. He taught me as well as led me to those who would assist and support me on my journey. Recently in a church service, I heard the Spirit say that my first book was to prepare me for now! Today is not yesterday, and a fresh anointing is needed to bring home the lost and restore truth and righteousness to our world. When the Spirit calls, step out in faith, listen to that still, small voice, and move in the anointed power of a Holy God. There is nothing impossible for a child of the King to achieve as long as you keep your mind and heart anchored on your Heavenly Father, the great I AM!

However, when He, the Spirit of truth, has come, He will guide you into all truth; for He will not speak on His own authority, but whatever He hears He will speak; and He will tell you things to come. 14He will glorify Me, for He will take of what is Mine and declare it to you. 15All things that the Father has are Mine. Therefore I said that He will take of Mine and declare it to you.

JOHN 16:13-15 NKJV

A Stirring

There is a stirring that is new and fresh. It is different from anything that we, the Body of Christ, have ever seen or heard from the past. This is a new day, a new awakening. The fire of the Spirit has been set, and it is purifying and refilling those who have learned to dwell in that secret place with the Father. This new thing will look and sound uniquely different. As the shaking intensifies, a sound emerges from the ashes - a wail, a cry for holiness, for righteousness, for a new man and woman to stand! This new man and woman will not compromise, not bow, and not live in fear but will rise up on eagle's wings and *soar*. This new voice will rest upon the Word of God and declare and decree the *power*, the *might*, and the *faithfulness* of Yeshua's Word. Adonai's hand will settle on this new man and woman, and then signs and wonders will follow.

The Lord is inviting His chosen ones to come back to that intimate place of worship and praise where a man or woman's heart and the great I AM's heart will merge together as One!

THE FIRE IN THE LORD'S EYES

Today as we were singing praises during our church service, there was a phrase that kept going through my mind. It was about the fire in our Lord's eyes. The Holy Spirit kept repeating that verse over and over to me. He reminded me of the power of fire. Fire burns, destroys, tears down, purifies, and cleanses. He said to me, "If the Body of Christ will allow My fire to cleanse, tear down, and purify each one so that he or she is ready to stand and battle; then My fire will go before each son and daughter, destroying every obstacle that the enemy places in his or her path. I will make their way straight, removing anything and all that would try to interfere with My purpose and will being accomplished." The Lord is telling the Body and anyone who will surrender completely to Him that His fire will purify each one, preparing them for the days ahead. There can *NOT* be any openings in our armor that would allow the enemy access. Only by total obedience can we be victorious in the battles and struggles that lie ahead. How do we increase our faith to believe? The Word states that faith comes by hearing the Word of God. (Rom. 10:17) Listen and obey is the message that the Spirit is speaking today. Allow the fire to do its work in you so that you can be prepared for the battle tomorrow and beyond. We walk in authority and power as long as our focus is above; our minds, our souls, and our bodies are under submission to the great I AM!

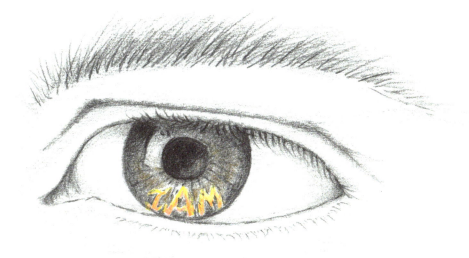

Dare to be a Daniel

Obedience   Righteousness   Purity

Each one supports <u>FAITH</u>.

If one is missing, faith cannot stand; and faith cannot grow!

FAITH RESTS UPON

| OBEDIENCE | PURITY | RIGHTEOUSNESS |

A Firm Foundation

| OBEDIENCE | Rage, Sin, Pride, Drugs, Lust, Greed, Unforgiveness, Pornography, Hate, Anger, Gossip, Envy | RIGHTEOUSNESS |

Foundation Built <> <> <> <> <> on Sinking Sand

PURITY

100 ~ Darla Colombo

Prophecy 2-23-20

I am going to pour out my wrath upon this world once again. Those who know Me – those who walk in obedience shall not fear. My wrath will be poured out on the disobedient – those who know My Truth but still deceive the lost - those who value money / profit over the truth of My Word. Only those who desire Me shall be protected. Search your heart. What idols have you placed in your heart? Don't you know … don't you perceive that there is only One who is worthy. There is only One that could be the redeemer of the lost – My Son, Jesus.

My Name will be elevated! My Name will be exalted! Every hidden lie, every hidden sin will be exposed by My Light. From the White House, from the highest court in the land, to every small government, to everyone who claims to be a child of the Most High – nothing hidden will remain. Cleanse your hearts, repent, and turn back to Me, or every hidden sin will be revealed.

My eyes search here and there looking for someone to stand in the gap – to intercede for the lost – to intercede for the sinner – to remind Me of My Word.

Judgement, judgement is coming, and it will begin with My house. So search your hearts. Where have you hidden your idols? Where have you compromised the Truth of My Word?

The greatest outpouring of My rain is coming. Only those whose hearts are pure will receive all that I have promised. So repent, you back sliders. Fall on your face and cry out for mercy before I close the door. Only by My Spirit can hearts be truly healed, delivered, and set free. The latter day rain will consume those who are ready. They will be My Mighty Warriors who go forth healing the sick, delivering the oppressed, and releasing those held bound by the enemy.

So My children, prepare, prepare, prepare for the greatest outpouring man has ever witnessed. But know that a mighty battle is coming. Put on your complete armor and be covered in prayer. Stand Strong … Do Not Fear because the Great I AM lives inside you. I have given you everything you need. My Angelic Army stands with you. Watch and listen to My Voice; knowing My Will shall be the key to success. Sanctify your ears to hear only My Voice. LISTEN, OBEY, and MOVE. Stand Strong – Stand Strong!

Faith and the Spoken Word

<u>Mat. 28:18</u>

And Jesus came and spoke to them, saying, "All authority has been given to Me in heaven and on earth.
<u>Luke 9:1-2</u>

Then He called His twelve disciples together and gave them power and authority over all demons, and to cure diseases. He sent them to preach the kingdom of God and to heal the sick.
<u>Eph. 1:18.20</u>

the eyes of your understanding being enlightened; that you may know what is the hope of His calling, what are the riches of the glory of His inheritance in the saints, and what is the exceeding greatness of His power toward us who believe, according to the working of His mighty power which He worked in Christ when He raised Him from the dead and seated Him at His right hand in the heavenly places

<u>Isa. 55:10-11</u>

"For as the rain comes down, and the snow from heaven,
And do not return there,
But water the earth,
And make it bring forth and bud,
That it may give seed to the sower
And bread to the eater,

So shall My word be that goes forth from My mouth;
It shall not return to Me void,
But it shall accomplish what I please,
And it shall prosper in the thing for which I sent it.

<u>Jer. 23:28-29</u>

"The prophet who has a dream, let him tell a dream;
And he who has My word, let him speak My word faithfully.
What *is* the chaff to the wheat?" says the LORD.

"Is not My word like a fire?" says the LORD,
"And like a hammer *that* breaks the rock in pieces?

My Identity in CHRIST

ACCEPTED – Eph. 1:6   LOVED – Eph. 1:4 / 2:4

ADOPTED – Eph. 1:5-6

FORGIVEN – Eph. 1:7   A CHILD of GOD – Romans 8:16

CHOSEN – John 15:16

COMPLETE – Col. 2:10   REDEEMED – Gal. 3:13

CARED FOR – 1 Peter: 5:7 / Jer. 29:11

BLESSED – Eph. 1:3   HEALED – 1Peter 2:24

A MASTERPIECE – Eph. 2:10

AN HEIR – Romans 8:17   A TEMPLE – 1Peter 2:5

MADE RIGHT with GOD – 2 Cor. 5:21

LED by the SPIRIT – Romans 8:14   A FRIEND of JESUS – John 15:14

DECLARED not GUILTY - Romans 3:24

NOT AFRAID – 2 TIM. 1:7   AN OVERCOMER – 1John 4:4 / Phil 4:13

VICTORIOUS – Romans 8:37

LIVING by FAITH – 2Cor. 5:7   STRONG in the LORD – Eph. 6:10 / Psalm 18:35

AN EXAMPLE – Eph. 5:1

SAVED by GRACE – Eph. 2:8

A CHRISTIAN IS ...

Joyful, Peaceful
STABLE

Righteous, Holy
STABLE

Kind
STABLE

Compassionate
STABLE

Merciful
STABLE

Faithful, Loyal
STABLE

Loving
STABLE

**STABLE* is established, fixed, sure, permanent, constant

*Taken from <u>Unshakeable</u> by John Eckhardt

How to Intercede

1. Repent if needed
2. Praise/Thanksgiving
3. Quiet yourself
4. USE your weapons:

A. *Put on the full armor of God* (Eph. 6:11-18) "Put on the whole armor of God, that you may be able to stand against the wiles of the devil. 12For we do not wrestle against flesh and blood, but against principalities, against powers, against the rulers of the darkness of this age, against spiritual hosts of wickedness in the heavenly places. 13Therefore take up the whole armor of God that you may be able to withstand in the evil day, and having done all, to stand.

14Stand therefore, having girded your waist with truth, having put on the breastplate of righteousness, 15and having shod your feet with the preparation of the gospel of peace; 16above all, taking the shield of faith with which you will be able to quench all the fiery darts of the wicked one. 17And take the helmet of salvation, and the sword of the Spirit, which is the word of God; 18praying always with all prayer and supplication in the Spirit, being watchful to this end with all perseverance and supplication for all the saints."

B. *Be strong* (Eph. 6:10) "Finally, my brethren, be strong in the Lord and in the power of His might."

C *Bind the enemy* (Matt. 18:18-20) " Assuredly, I say to you, whatever you bind on earth will be bound in heaven, and whatever you loose on earth will be loosed in heaven.

19 Again I say to you that if two of you agree on earth concerning anything that they ask, it will be done for them by My Father in heaven. 20For where two or three are gathered together in My name, I am there in the midst of them."

D. *Resist the devil* (James 4:7) "Therefore submit to God. Resist the devil and he will flee from you."

E. *Claim the blood* (Rev. 12:11) "And they overcame him by the blood of the Lamb and by the word of their testimony, and they did not love their lives to the death."

F. *Loose the captive* (Luke 4:18) "The Spirit of the Lord is upon Me,

Because He has anointed Me
To preach the gospel to the poor;
He has sent Me to heal the brokenhearted,
To proclaim liberty to the captives
And recovery of sight to the blind,
To set at liberty those who are oppressed;
19To proclaim the acceptable year of the Lord."

G. *Pull down strongholds* (2 Cor. 10:3-5) "For though we walk in the flesh, we do not war according to the flesh. 4For the weapons of our warfare are not carnal but mighty in God for pulling down strongholds, 5casting down arguments and every high thing that exalts itself against the knowledge of God, bringing every thought into captivity to the obedience of Christ."

H. *Make a hedge of protection* (Eze. 22:30) "So I sought for a man among them who would make a wall, and stand in the gap before Me on behalf of the land, that I should not destroy it; but I found no one."

I. *Command him to leave* (Matt. 10:1) "And when He had called His twelve disciples to Him, He gave them power over unclean spirits, to cast them out, and to heal all kinds of sickness and all kinds of disease."

J. *Rebuke him (demon) in Jesus's Name* (Matt. 17:18) "And Jesus rebuked the demon, and it came out of him; and the child was cured from that very hour."

Remember praying in your prayer language is one of the most powerful weapons you have!

PRAYER

A Conduit to the Power of a Holy God

Prayer rests upon the foundational stone, Jesus Christ, of our faith. Nothing is accomplished in our walk with our Father if it is not first bathed in prayer. We are in a season of intense warfare and must know how to stand and how to battle using our spiritual weapons to bring God's will into this earthly realm.

> Ephesians 6:18 "praying always with all prayer and supplication in the Spirit, being watchful to this end with all perseverance and supplication for all the saints." NKJV

In this scripture according to Strong's Concordance #G3956, <u>all</u> prayer means all forms of prayer. There is no formula prayer for each and every situation. Only the Holy Spirit knows what the will of the Father is. Our prayers must be Spirit-led and Spirit-directed. When one studies Ephesians 6:18, he or she begins to understand what Saint Paul is saying to the church at Ephesus. <u>In</u> the Spirit, #G1722, means a fixed position. We are in Christ, and He is in us if we are saved and walking in obedience. Disobedience takes us out of that fixed position where our prayers are not heard.

> "If I regard iniquity in my heart, the Lord will not hear."
> Psalm 66:18 NKJV

> "Now we know that God does not hear sinners; but if anyone is a worshiper of God and does His will, He hears him".
> John 9:31 NKJV

In the beginning of Ephesians Chapter 6, Paul tells the church to put on the whole armor that God provides. This armor enables us to stand and fight the lies and deceptions of the enemy. Verse 12 emphasizes that we do not battle against the flesh and blood of humans but against the principalities and powers who rule in spiritual darkness. Two weapons the Roman soldiers used in battle were the spear and the lance. Depending on the battle, the weapon chosen would vary in size, shape, and even length. This is the same with prayer. God has given the body of Christ powerful tools of prayer to destroy strongholds, to tear down lies of deception, to break chains that bind, and to deliver and set free those held in bondage.

Following is a portion of the spiritual weapons of prayer with corresponding scriptures:

>Praying the Word – Hebrews 4:12
>Praying the Name – John 14:14; Luke 10:17
>Praying in the Spirit/Tongues – Romans 8:26-27
>Praying the Blood – Revelations 12:11
>Prayer of Faith – James 5:13-15
>Prayer of Intercession – Ezekiel 22:30
>Prayer of Supplication – Philippians 4:6
>Prayer of Petition – 1Timothy 2:1-4
>Prayer of Consecration – Matthew 26:39
>Prayer of Thanksgiving – Psalm 100:4
>Prayer of Agreement – Matthew 18:19
>Prayer of Authority – John 15:7
>Prayer of Binding and Loosing – Matthew 18:18-19

Each weapon is effective but must be directed by the Holy Spirit. In Romans 8:26-27, the Word states, "Likewise the Spirit also helps in our weaknesses. For we do not know what we should pray for as we ought, but the spirit Himself makes intercession for us with groanings which cannot be uttered. Now he who searches the hearts knows what the mind of the Spirit is, because He makes intercession for the saints according to the will of God." NKJV According to Strong's Concordance of definitions, we can get a better understanding of what Paul is telling the saints at Rome. The word <u>helpeth</u>, #G4878, means to take hold of or to cooperate or assist; <u>infirmities/ weaknesses</u>, #G769, means feebleness of mind or body; and <u>intercession</u>, #G5241, means to intercede on behalf of or to fall into with. It is the idea of the Holy Spirit coming alongside us or meeting with us as we pray. Since we don't know what God's plan or purpose is, the Holy Spirit comes to our aid and joins us in our prayers. He actually rescues us and prays the perfect will of the Father for that specific situation.

Spiritual warfare prayer is a powerful tool against Satan's plans and devices. One of the most effective prayers is praying the Word of God. "For the word of God is living and powerful, and sharper than any two-edged sword, piercing even to the division of soul and spirit, and of joints and marrow, and is a discerner of the thoughts and intents of the heart." Hebrews 4:12 NKJV In order for a prayer to hit the bulls-eye, one must know and have stored in his or her heart God's Holy Word.

The Bible is the only book ever written that is God-breathed total TRUTH! "Sanctify them [purify, consecrate, separate them for Yourself, make them holy] by the Truth; Your Word is Truth." John 17:17 AMPC When we decree audibly God's Word, we are proclaiming to the demonic world the Father's perfect will, plan, and purpose in each circumstance. You may ask, "Why do I need to speak or declare the Word audibly rather than just thinking or praying it?" Man was created in the image and likeness of God (Genesis 1:26). In Hebrew the word image is tselem #G6754, means a representative of. Then the scripture states after our likeness #H1823, which means resemblance, like manner. However, God did not stop there but declared that man was to have dominion over the fish of the sea, the fowl of the air, the cattle, and over all the earth. Dominion is an interesting Hebrew word, radah. Radah's definition, #H7287, is to tread down, to subjugate, to rule over, or to reign over. If we, man/woman, are made in the image and likeness of our Heavenly Father and are to have dominion over the earth, we need to emulate our Creator. When God the Father created, He SPOKE! In Genesis 1:3 He said, "Let there be", and it came into existence.

If the Word is Truth and if we are made in the image and likeness of our Creator and are to have dominion, then that same anointing is upon the body of Christ to declare and decree God's perfect will in our families, our nation, and our world. "So shall My word be that goes forth out of My mouth: it shall not return to Me void [without producing any effect, useless], but it shall accomplish that which I please and purpose, and it shall prosper in the thing for which I sent it." Isaiah 55:11. AMPC This scripture explains the power of the spoken Word of God. The Word mixed with faith enables the arrow to hit the target each time. As I was preparing to teach on the subject of prayer at my church, the Spirit spoke these words to me.

> "You can't be in agreement (with the Word), if you are not walking in obedience. And if you are not walking in obedience, then you can't have faith to believe."

This strengthens the Lord's Truth that obedience is required not only to have our prayers answered but also to have the faith to believe. Without faith, how can a Christian possibly trust in God's Holy Word? Faith and the Word are intertwined. One can't exist without the other!

Coming alongside the spoken Word is the angelic host. Psalm 103:20 explains that angels do the Father's commands and hearken unto the voice of His word. KJV Angels watch us and listen to the words we speak. They are ministering spirits that are ever ready to hear and follow God's voice. When we, the body of Christ, decree His Holy Word, angels respond. Declaring the Word of God audibly mobilizes the host of Heaven to bring that Word into existence. Remember the words we speak produce either life or death. Speak life!

Probably the most powerful, crucial weapon of prayer given to the believer is praying in our prayer language. Several scriptures speak about this spiritual weapon that was given to the body of Christ to intercede and stand in the gap.

> "But you, my delightfully loved friends, constantly and progressively build yourselves up on the foundation of your most holy faith by praying every moment in the Spirit." Jude 1:20 TPT

> "When someone speaks in tongues, no one understands a word he says, because he's not speaking to people, but to God—he is speaking intimate mysteries in the Spirit." 1 Cor. 14:2 TPT

> "But when the truth-giving Spirit comes, he will unveil the reality of every truth within you. He won't speak on his own, but only what he hears from the Father, and he will reveal

prophetically to you what is to come. 14He will glorify me on the earth, for he will receive from me what is mine and reveal it to you." John 16:13-14 TPT

John 4:24 declares that God is a spiritual Being, and we must worship Him in the realm of Spirit and Truth. Knowing the limits of humankind, the Lord sent the gift of the Holy Spirit to equip us and aid us in our journey in this earthly realm. Since we are made in three parts, spirit, soul, and body, the Lord provided a way in which we can speak to God, spirit to spirit. Our spiritual language comes to our aid and prays with and through us the perfect prayer. He, the Holy Spirit, comes alongside each son and daughter and beseeches the Father on our behalf. Through the Holy Spirit we are seated in heavenly places and pray from a location that is above principalities and powers. Thus, we pray from a position of authority and victory.

Recently I read a book, <u>70 Reasons to Pray in Tongues</u>, by Dr. Bill Hamon. Even though I have been spirit-filled for over forty years, the Holy Spirit knew that I needed to strengthen this gift for the days ahead. We have crossed the threshold into a new era of time. Praying under the leadership and direction of the Holy Spirit is urgently needed. In Acts 1 Jesus told the disciples to wait for the Promise of the Father. Being baptized with the Holy Spirit would clothe the disciples with power, boldness, and wisdom.

As Christ's representatives we are commissioned to be the Voice and the Light in this earthly realm. Praying in our prayer language not only builds the faith of each Christian but also allows the Spirit to pray the perfect will of God through him or her. One of the most interesting lessons I have learned while reading Dr. Bill Hamon's book is that when we pray in our prayer language, we pray at the speed of light. Since God is Light and the Holy Spirit is Light, praying in tongues connects our spirit man with God and functions in this same dimension of light. That means we can achieve more in a few minutes of spirit-led prayer then we could accomplish in hours of praying in our own natural ability. Then Jesus said, "I am light to the world, and those who embrace me will experience life-giving light, and they will never walk in darkness." John 8:12 TPT

When we pray in our prayer language with other believers at the same time for the same thing, we pray in unity. Our emotions and our thoughts have no impact on our prayer. In Leviticus 26:8 the Word states, "Five of you shall chase a hundred, and a hundred of you shall put ten thousand to flight; your enemies shall fall before you by the sword." AMPC These soldiers were unified and fighting as one. Thus, true unified prayer can only be fulfilled when spirit-led believers come together and pray in their prayer language at the same time. A greater power is released as more and more Christians bind together. Imagine if the world-wide church merged together and prayed in their prayer language at the same time, how many demonic strongholds would be destroyed and torn down. What a victory for our Lord.

Growing and becoming more like our Savior is another benefit bestowed on each son and daughter as he or she prays in tongues. Remember Jude 1:20 "But you, my delightfully loved friends, constantly and progressively build yourselves up on the foundation of your most holy faith by praying every moment in the Spirit." This Word reveals that praying in our prayer language helps each person grow in his or her spiritual walk and be transformed into Christ's image. The more we pray, the more we become; the more we become, the more we fulfill God's calling and destiny for our lives.

In addition, as we pray in our prayer language, our spiritual gifts are activated and manifested in the same manner in the natural realm.

> "But to each one is given the manifestation of the [Holy] Spirit [the evidence, the spiritual illumination of the Spirit] for good and profit.
>
> 8 To one is given in and through the [Holy] Spirit [the power to speak] a message of wisdom, and to another [the power to express] a word of knowledge and understanding according to the same [Holy] Spirit;

9 To another [wonder-working] faith by the same [Holy] Spirit, to another the extraordinary powers of healing by the one Spirit;

10 To another the working of miracles, to another prophetic insight (the gift of interpreting the divine will and purpose); to another the ability to discern and distinguish between [the utterances of true] spirits [and false ones], to another various kinds of [unknown] tongues, to another the ability to interpret [such] tongues.

11 All these [gifts, achievements, abilities] are inspired and brought to pass by one and the same [Holy] Spirit, Who apportions to each person individually [exactly] as He chooses." 1 Cor. 12:7-11 AMPC

These are just two of the powerful spiritual weapons of prayer that Yahweh has given His church. Study each one and allow the Spirit to use you in life-changing prayer. Fear is a tactic of the enemy that is used to stop the power and anointing of the body. Don't fear but pray. Use your tools from the Lord. Stand, fight, and believe!

DOROTHY POST KERNS-SWICK

BIOGRAPHY

Dorothy is a watercolor artist residing in Clarksburg, West Virginia. She was born in Texas where her father, while stationed in the Army, met her mother. Transplanted to West Virginia as a small child, she has grown to love both her West Virginia and Texas heritages. Twice married, both husbands having gone on to glory, she is the proud mother of adult biological and step children who are the absolute joy and blessings of her life. This blessing doubled with four incredible grandchildren and now three great-grandchildren. Blessings upon blessings!

Dorothy accepted the Lord as Savior when she was 12 years old. She admits to imperfections but is always thankful that the Lord has never let her stray far from His reach. Currently, she attends Lifepointe Church in Clarksburg.

As an artist, Dorothy states she cannot remember NOT being able to draw. She has studied on both a college level and with private instruction but is quick to tell everyone that she is primarily God-trained. She is both amazed and humbled at the ability He is able to bring forth through her. "I hold the brush, and the Lord paints" is often her response when someone complements her work. Dorothy taught art classes for 22 years at a West Virginia asthma camp for children, Camp Catch Your Breath. This camp was sponsored by United Hospital Center where Dorothy was employed for approximately 40 years. After several years of not being active artistically, the Lord began reigniting the gift in her through a good friend and owner of her local quilt shop. In 2015 she was asked to provide paintings of West Virginia wildflowers for a state quilting group, and again in 2016 they requested images of West Virginia birds. Both years these images were used to produce quilt fabric which was then sold throughout the state. Being both a quilter and a painter, Dorothy was amazed that the Lord presented her with such a unique opportunity. In 2018 in an effort to provide a special gift for a friend's birthday, she tried a new watercolor technique of painting on a used, dried, emptied teabag. At the time of this writing, she has painted 328 teabags, most of which have been used as "blessing gifts" to those the Lord puts on her heart. With this reigniting of her original artistic gift, Dorothy feels the Lord was ultimately preparing her for the time she would be asked to join in the work of providing illustrations for this unique book the Lord has given Darla to write. He has raised her artistry up "for Such a Time as This". James 1:17 states, "All good and perfect gifts come down from the Father of lights", and His timing is perfect.

CPSIA information can be obtained
at www.ICGtesting.com
Printed in the USA
JSHW041421260123
36573JS00010B/40